Chelsea, 1981

SKINHEADS!

1979 - 1984

Cover designed by Paul Tippett for Vitamin P
Book designed by Paul Tippett and Adrian Andrews for Vitamin P
All photographs by Derek Ridgers
Cover photo: Chelsea, 1981

ISBN: 978.1.78305.171.7
Order No: OP 55473

Exclusive Distributors
Music Sales Limited,
14/15 Berners Street,
London, W1T 3LJ

Music Sales Corporation
180 Madison Avenue, 24th Floor,
New York,
NY 10016,
USA

Macmillan Distribution Services,
56 Parkwest Drive
Derrimut, Vic 3030,
Australia

Printed in the EU.

A catalogue record for this book is available from the British Library.

Visit Omnibus Press on the web at www.omnibuspress.com.

I'd like to thank every one of the skinheads pictured in the following pages.

I'd also like to thank Andrew Bunney, David Chandler, Susan Compo, Danny Flynn, Marcus Georgiou, Carrie Kania, Babette Kulik, Victoria Lukens, Gordon MacDonald, Rupert Smyth and Professor Val Williams for all their help and advice over the years.

This book is dedicated to my wife Jo-Anne.

I'd also like to dedicate it to the memory of Andrew Heard and David Robillard – gone but certainly not forgotten guys.

www.derekridgers.com

SKINHEADS

1979 - 1984

Derek Ridgers

OMNIBUS PRESS

London / New York / Paris / Sydney / Copenhagen / Berlin / Madrid / Tokyo

Shoreditch, 1979

FOREWORD

Many of Derek Ridgers' skinhead photos play to the common understanding of skinheads. There is the camaraderie, yes, but there is also the aggression. It is remarkable just how many of the youths in Ridgers' shots seem to have their fists clenched, assuming, that is, they're not giving their 'sieg heil' salute.

One photo of a skinhead in Shoreditch, taken in 1979, seems to sum up everything that made the skinhead a folk devil: there is the haircut, of course, which the post-hippy fashions of the times considered anti-socially short, almost a parody of the neat, services-friendly haircut; there are those boots, which almost dominate the entire photo, so completely unavoidable, almost comedically outsized as they are; and there is the Nazi regalia – although not definitively a skinhead trope, seeing how punk too had dabbled with its utterly outré symbolism – is unusually unsubtle, being emblazoned across his T-shirt and all over his jacket, which, of course, takes punk's playfulness over the edge by adding in the badges of a more straightforwardly unpleasant ideology too.

But maybe most striking of all is the young man's face, chiseled into a frown that is part anger, part frustration and, more than that, in large part quizzical. It is as though he doesn't really know what he represents, whether he is part of something or simply cut off from the greater something else, why he is the way he is, or where he should be going. Maybe he knows just one thing for sure: that he is a skinhead.

That is one reading at least. Perhaps the subject of the photo would tell a story of belonging and self-confidence and laser-guided hatred – hatred of others, of elders, of a society which was, lest we forget, then uneducated in political correctness, facing seismic social change and about as close to the end of the Second World War as Brits today are, for example, to the Falklands War – which hints at just how viscerally, caustically offensive that Nazi imagery would have been.

Times were tough, a counter to the supposed boom years of the 1980s just around the corner: unemployment was high, strikes were regular, government ineffective and – in part out of a Commonwealth debt, in part because the labour was needed in the UK and partly because the nation offered a better life – immigration was rising.

More sympathetically understood, with hindsight one can see how skinheads were no more – and no less – than an expression of youthful angst in a troubled era. They were the 1970s' answer to the sweat-panted and hoodie-topped youths that haunted council estates and, with others, rioted across east London in 2011 – only arguably much less hateful, in every sense.

Of course, the skinhead was just that: a folk devil – a concept introduced by sociologist Stanley Cohen during the same decade as the skinheads' greatest prominence; indeed, although the concept was inspired by earlier mods and rockers, its arrival was perfectly timed for the skinheads.

The folk devil was the subject of a media-fueled moral panic, blamed for rising crime, bouts of personal violence and perceived as an organised threat to society's moral norms – precisely the norms that, after an exuberant teens and early twenties, most members of said folk devilry normally joined quite peaceably, tattoos or not.

This is not to say there were not problems, even if the skinhead's bad reputation was over-played throughout the 1970s and early 1980s,

both by the media and in a series of popular if controversial skinhead novels by Richard Allen – some of which sold in excess of a million copies – in which fighting, and fighting with racist intent at that, was a key event. Gigs with post-punk bands like The Angelic Upstarts, Cockney Rejects, Cock Sparrer and, best known of all,

Sham 69 – the purveyors of 'oi!' – offered stories of real life on British streets and the marginalisation faced by working class British youth that appealed to the skin sensibility, but also risked turning into brawls between skinheads and whoever was there who happened, unfortunately, to not be a skinhead. Such was the problem that bands with genuine potential lost bookings and record deals. Slade – now best known for its Christmas anthem – was an exception, beginning as a skinhead band, or rather being persuaded by its

management to appeal to skinheads by aping their style, but escaping to, of all things, glam rock, in its costume of excesses and escapism which was arguably skinhead's polar opposite.

Football was to skinheads as coffee bars, seafronts and scooters were to the Mods, which is to say a kind of social glue. It was also a flashpoint.

THEY WERE THE 1970s' ANSWER TO THE SWEAT-PANTED AND HOODIE-TOPPED YOUTHS THAT HAUNTED COUNCIL ESTATES AND, WITH OTHERS, RIOTED ACROSS EAST LONDON IN 2011 – ONLY ARGUABLY MUCH LESS HATEFUL...

Despite the confiscation of one's laces, even of the entire perceived potential weapon that was one's steel toe-capped boots, it was not unknown for a skinhead set on violence to carry a comb with sharpened handle – not the most obvious accessory for the follicularly denuded – or even just a newspaper, less for reading than for rolling and folding into a so-called Millwall Brick, a kind of DIY cosh named after the notorious London football club. There is no denying that there was skinhead trouble, and that some skinheads were troubled.

But the fact is that, for all that the skinhead was a provocateur, fought in the streets ruined – in the view of some – football as a family affair and got scooter rallies campaigned against across the UK, he was not aggressive beyond anything that might be regarded as the high jinks of excess testosterone, which had been seen before, and which has been seen since.

Sadly, that notion is mostly lost: the bad apples of skinhead seemingly have tarnished the name irretrievably. In fact, they continue to shape public perception of this youth movement even today – just getting a closely cropped hairstyle is to invite the impression that you are not to be trusted. Incredibly, so mistrusted was the hairstyle that US servicemen stationed in Britain during the period – and whose regulation haircuts resembled that of skinheads – were granted permission to wear a hairpiece when socialising off-base, so as to help them avoid either trouble or approbation.

So powerful is this negative stereotype that it was archly played on by a TV advertisement for *The Guardian* newspaper in 1986, which showed an archetypal skin running full-pelt down a road towards a briefcase-carrying gent, who he then man-handles to the ground. Every angle leads viewers to the impression that the skin has just mugged an innocent victim. *The Guardian's* view, the ad suggests, reveals the truth: the skin has just pushed the man out of the way of falling scaffolding.

Certainly for most within the movement – if it can be called that – being a skinhead was apolitical, a unifying sharing of a style and taste that, like most youth tribes, provided a sense of identity for the mostly white, mostly male, mostly working class and (while skinheads, many of the far right persuasion, could be found in the US, in Greece and in Germany too, among other places) mostly British displaced youth. Like tribes before and after, clothes, music and sport proved a powerful bonding agent. This is the skinhead of Ridgers' photo of three skins hanging around Charing Cross, taken in 1979 – little more than school kids in their identikit out-of-school uniforms, part modern-day urchins, part wannabe lads on the town, but largely, one imagines, innocent of anything they would regret in later life.

It is their more simply tribal notion of skinhead that should have been the one to have lasting resonance – skinhead as youth phenomenon, as an often sharp street style. Indeed, skinhead was arguably the last fashion-based youth tribe of any real

LIKE TRIBES BEFORE AND AFTER, CLOTHES, MUSIC AND SPORT PROVED A POWERFUL BONDING AGENT.

significance in the UK. The Casuals who followed through the 1980s were deeply regionalised and barely noticed by the media at large, and British youth has since been seemingly disparate, fractured further by the possibilities of the internet and, to many older generations' eyes, appeared rather unimaginatively disheveled.

Forty or so years ago that in itself might have been considered an offensive idea to many a skin – perhaps nothing was so fey, so unblokey (and all the more so for such a blokey scene) as a consideration for the way one dressed.

Outside Charing Cross station, 1979

Leicester Square, 1981

Brick Lane, 1980

Brick Lane, 1980

Of course, skinheads might argue that their garb was entirely functional – a kind of battle dress for the streets: the haircut, for example, made hair hard to grab in a fist fight. But on a closer look it is hard to deny that, for all of its sometimes cartoonish machismo, the look of the skinhead was a deeply considered, even narcissistic one. Ridgers' shot of a skinhead couple, taken on London's Brick Lane in 1980 – the man cupping his girlfriend's breast – reveals just what a carefully assembled style it was, however utilitarian, accessible and 'man of the people' its components. With his polished, 12-hole Docs, with their red laces, cropped and turned-up

Levi's Red Tab jeans, his matching trucker jacket and button-down shirt – even with the characterful gap between his front teeth – the man is practically a fashion plate. His girlfriend pays attention to the details too, from her white socks to clip-on braces – of a narrow width only please – through to feathered fringe and her polo shirt in West Ham colours. It is hard to deny that they look 'cool' in a way recognisable to 21st-century eyes. This was the skinhead's proudly British working class idea of always being in presentable dress, a notion that their parents might recognise even if they might not appreciate the results.

Much has gone unappreciated. What most people who take the folk-devil line in their understanding of skinhead, for example, also might not appreciate are the deeper origins of the tribe. Their view is typically shaped by the media image of the later stages of the movement – as is also reflected in much of Ridgers' skinhead work.

This was, to some extent, after skinhead had exploded – at least, sufficiently enough to catch media attention for the first real time. Yet skinhead can actually date its beginnings back to the 1960s and the tail-end of mod, of which it is a stylistic close relative.

Certainly the pioneers of the skinhead look – and this was long before skinhead even became a self-defining term, long before Prime Minister Harold Wilson used the nomenclature in the House of Commons (and he wasn't doing so in praise) – were known as 'hard mods'. The boots were already part of the style, the haircuts then more extreme takes on the Modish French crew-cut, such that they would also be dubbed 'lemons', 'peanuts', 'crop-heads' or 'boiled eggs' – none of them terms for a collective style that was likely to ever catch on. And the style they pioneered, to which many of Ridgers' photos attest, could be exacting, but

culminated in that most skinhead of attributes: pride and swagger. There were the uncompromising haircuts and the jeans – always rolled, sometimes splashed with bleach. And there were also the boots, of course, with that preference for steel toe-capped army boots – or, later, Doc Marten's – the leather perhaps worn through at the toe to reveal either the shine of the metal below, not unlike that of many a skin's shaved skull, or black, into which might be rubbed oxblood polish to create an aging effect, with the laces worn tied around the top of the boot, fed through the pull tab at the rear, and colour-coded (with white laces suggesting supremacist leanings).

Near The Last Resort in Goulston Street, Aldgate, 1981

Shirts were in Oxford cloth, plain, striped or, later, checked – gingham was a favourite – with button-down collars a relatively late addition to the dress rule book. Braces, for show rather than actual support, were some kind of statement of working class solidarity – perhaps of something considered quintessentially British – and tended to hoist jeans up beyond the realms of comfort, so were often worn loose around the hips.

One favoured jacket – like the haircut, a style that would remain tarnished by skinhead associations for decades to come – was the 'flightie' or MA1 nylon flight jacket, often in black rather than the standard issue olive green.

In style terms at least, skinhead women perhaps got the short end of the stick, as some of Ridgers' images suggest: some might wear a black mini-skirt with ripped tights, loafers and white socks, but skin style for them was essentially a scaled-down version of what was in essence a very male code of attire. What Ridgers' photos suggest is what a minority women were anyway – unlike many other youth tribes, from mod to punk and new romanticism – a skinhead girl was typically present either as a partner to another solitary skin, or in the safe company of a girlfriend and be considered the first youth tribe to be determined, sartorially-speaking, by an obsessive regard for certain brands, cheaper alternatives were never shunned providing the overall look was adhered to. Membership was what mattered. Never mind if your jeans were from Brutus and not Levi's – you wore them short, like a badge.

THERE WERE THE UNCOMPROMISING HAIRCUTS AND THE JEANS – ALWAYS ROLLED, SOMETIMES SPLASHED WITH BLEACH.

vastly outnumbered by a leery male pack. Perhaps the clothes put most off, perhaps the loutishness.

But there was also the skinhead's predilection for certain labels – button-down shirts were ideally by Ben Sherman ('Bennies', as they became known), polo shirts were by Fred Perry, loafers or brogues by Faith Royal and coats by Crombie. And although skinhead might arguably

And that fact alone hints at something more shockingly revelatory still, at least as far as the stereotype goes: skinhead's first founding, cultural inspirations. The cropped trousers were said to have been worn, although not consciously by most skinheads admittedly, in imitation of a Jamaican street style popularised in 1967 by Desmond Dekker – a black musician.

East London, 1981

Hounslow bus station, 1980

Shoreditch, 1979

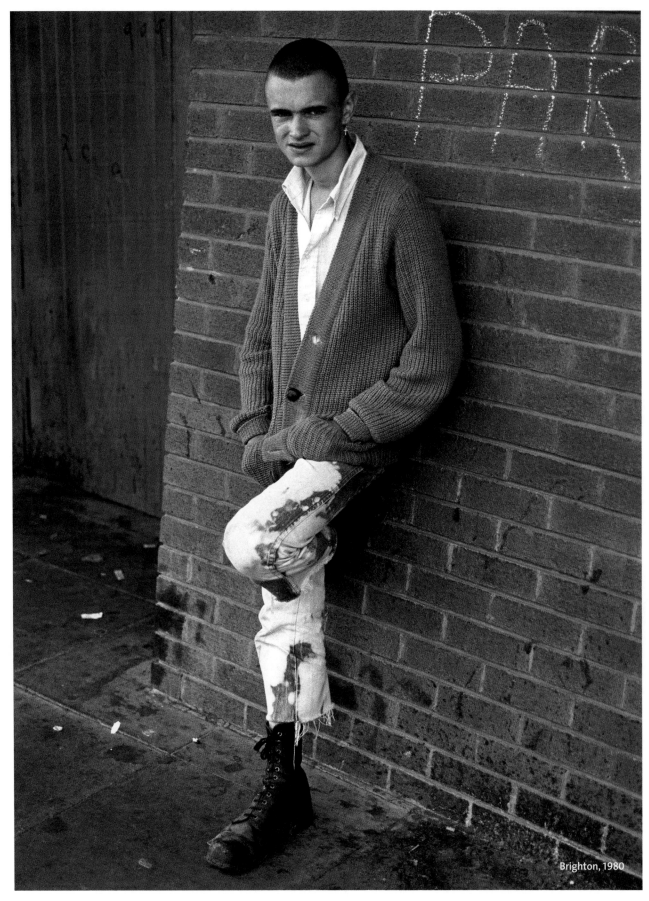

Brighton, 1980

And the music skinheads first danced to, in the 1960s? Thanks in part to the records brought over by US servicemen, they included the then still rather underground genres of American soul and Jamaican reggae – black music.

Indeed, before barely understood right-wing extremism, the silly scowls and one finger salutes became a default setting for skinhead, the relationship between it and black music culture was mutually appreciative. Among the songs tripping off the records from labels such as Island and Trojan were the likes of the 'Skinhead Shuffle', 'Skinhead Train' and 'Skinhead Moonstomp'. The ska inflection in the style of the skinhead with the Madness button on his jacket, or in the skinhead group of four in Ridgers' photo taken in London's Stoke Newington area in 1981 – the pork-pie

House party in Stoke Newington, 1981

hat, the flat caps, the novelty sunglasses, not to mention the presence of a black man – makes that clearer still.

These are what, in contrast to those hard mods, one might call the 'soft skins', and are what skinhead became: the style not so extreme, the nationalism now more patriotism, the scowl now more cheeky chappy grin. In other words, while it continued in more adult form abroad, in the UK skinhead more clearly reverted to what it had, at heart, always meant to be about, and which is best encapsulated by Ridgers' image of a train interior packed with bright eyes and broad smiles one bank holiday in 1979: lads having fun and being young together.

Josh Sims
February 2014

Contact sheet. Southend, 1979

SKINPRINtS

This didn't start out as a project. I never intended to photograph the skinheads at all. It came about completely by accident...

Back in the 1970s, I was an advertising agency art director with easy access to a camera. By night I was a keen music fan and I'd started taking a camera to gigs, forcing my way to the front and shooting photos of some of the bands I liked.

In the beginning, I was just pretending to be a photographer. It was simply an excuse to get a bit closer to the musicians themselves. But I also started to quite enjoy printing the photographs I'd taken.

In 1976, punk happened. You had to be blind not to see how photogenic the punks were and so I turned the attention of my camera around and began to photograph the audience as well as the bands. And even though I was an amateur and my photographs weren't really very good, magazines and newspapers were clamouring for images of what the media considered the big new youth craze.

I printed all my photographs myself at home, using our tiny larder and with all the chemicals arranged in plastic cat-litter trays. Our larder was so small, even with all the cans of food removed, that there was only just enough room for me to stand up. I even had to put a lock on the inside of the door to prevent me from leaning back slightly and pinging it open, letting the light in and therefore exposing the prints.

Nevertheless, my photos were quite successful.

It was pure beginner's luck, helped by the photos being timely and available. And because of my advertising background, I had chutzpah and was fairly shameless in touting them around.

My punk photographs were used on the cover of the now iconic LP *100 Nights At The Roxy* and extensively in the book of the same name.

They were shown at London's Institute of Contemporary Arts and printed in several photography magazines, including the prestigious *Zoom*. After which, I decided I wanted to consolidate my success and find other youth groups to photograph. I didn't have to wait long.

Early in 1978 I read about a club in Soho called Billy's, where teenagers were dressing up in really flamboyant and eccentric clothes and dancing to David Bowie and Kraftwerk records. It was almost the complete antithesis of the austerity and anti-fashion ethos of punk. Almost, but not quite.

Like the punks, there was still a strong element of DIY evident in many of the outfits. But this lot looked to be even more photogenic than the punks, so I went down to Billy's and started to document them as well.

The kids in that club turned out to be the first of the youth cult that became known as the New Romantics or, later on, the Blitz Kids.

To begin with, I was very much an outsider. They didn't particularly want me and my camera there. Steve Strange, the majordomo, often used to keep me waiting outside in the street for ages. But I was persistent and knew I'd get nowhere by taking "no" for an answer.

Once inside, the New Romantics were all so extrovert and desperate to be seen that they couldn't quite help presenting themselves for my camera. And it was certainly worth the wait.

At the age I was then, 27, I very much felt that my ship had sailed as far as being a punk or a New Romantic myself. I thought I was far too old for any of that nonsense. Therefore I never tried to present myself as anything other than just an observer with a camera.

By 1979 the original Billy's crowd had moved on but, as I wasn't one of the in-crowd, I was a little late in finding out. I turned up at Billy's one night, camera eagerly in hand, expecting to photograph the New Romantics, but they'd gone.

Leaving a few of the not quite so cool kids, a handful of tourists, a group

THE SKINHEADS WERE PRETTY FRIENDLY WHEN THEY SAW ME WITH MY CAMERA AND SUGGESTED I TAKE A FEW PHOTOS OF THEM.

of about half a dozen skinheads and one photographer.

The skinheads were pretty friendly when they saw me with my camera and suggested I take a few photos of them, which I did.

The de facto skinhead leader seemed to be a ginger-haired extrovert called Wally. He informed me that if I really wanted some good photographs, I should tag along in a few weeks' time when he and all his skinhead friends would be going to Southend for a Bank Holiday day out.

Wally, Embankment, 1979

On the train going to Southend, 1979

I must have been pretty daft. At first I assumed that Wally and his friends were just dressing up as skinheads. I thought that they'd probably all come from art schools or fashion colleges and they were benign, skinhead revivalists. I'd been a sort of low rent, cheapo version of a skinhead once myself in the Sixties, but I hadn't seen any in London for ages. I thought skinheads had long died out.

I proved to be seriously misinformed.

When the day of the Bank Holiday came, I met Wally and his friends at 8.00 a.m. at Fenchurch Street Station. By the time the train was nearing its departure, the number of skinheads milling around on the concourse had grown to about 30 or 40, including a few skinhead girls.

On the way to Southend, I took photographs of Wally and his friends and all the other skinheads in our carriage. None of them seemed to mind. I chatted to many of them and they acted like a bunch of cheerful, polite but fairly boisterous teenagers. They weren't being any more rowdy than any other group of young people on a day out would be. Probably less so than some.

But it was when I sat down and had a proper conversation with a few of

Wally, Hyde Park, 1979

them that I got a real eye opener. Without any prompting, they expressed an odd and rather extreme view of what being British meant to them: anti-semitism, a dislike of immigrants and homosexuals, and a very old-fashioned view of women's place in society. And they all seemed in complete accord, both male and female.

It was a set of views that I'd never personally encountered before.

And some of them seemed a little confused. They spoke about immigrants coming over to Britain and "taking our jobs" but, at the same time, they seemed to view those same immigrants as work shy and lazy.*

I have to say I was rather shocked. I can think of no better, no more accurate word than that – shocked. Maybe if I'd taken time out to study all the NF and British Movement T-shirts and badges many of them wore, or if I'd examined some of their tattoos, it wouldn't have come as such a surprise.

I was truthfully shocked. But it didn't put me off wanting to photograph them. Far from it. I decided I wanted to interview them as well, because I thought there might be a good story waiting to be told.

---

*In the fullness of time, I came to find out that Wally wasn't his real name and he was an immigrant himself. He recently emailed me and told me that he got deported to Australia.

Walking down to the seafront, Southend, 1979

By the time we arrived at Southend, somehow the number of skinheads had swelled and about 80 got off the train. As we all walked through the town towards the seafront, there were several groups of policemen watching us from a distance.

I continued to take photographs without anyone objecting – apart from one skinhead, who walked straight over and, without saying a single word, kicked me right between the legs.

I managed to twist slightly, right at the last moment, so that his boot didn't connect properly with my groin.

Thankfully. Then he tried to wrestle my camera from me. I hung on and after a bit of grappling he gave up. None of

HE SAID THAT HE OBJECTED TO ME BEING AROUND BECAUSE HE THOUGHT I WAS TAKING PHOTOGRAPHS FOR THE POLICE.

the other skinheads came to my aid and I saw some of them looking over and laughing.

I asked the guy what his problem was and, in a thick Scottish brogue that I could barely understand, he said that he objected to me being around

because he thought I was taking photographs for the police. I managed to disabuse him of this and, after a bit

of persuasion, he agreed to let me take some quick photos of him and the skinhead girl he was with. They still weren't being particularly friendly, but they were a great looking pair and my persistence had paid off. After which we all continued on our way.

Southend, Easter Bank Holiday, 1979

It was a warm, sunny day and, by the time we got down to the seafront, there was a tangible atmosphere of expectation. Added to the normal family groups one always gets at the seaside, members of most of the other youth tribes then current in the UK were starting to arrive too.

Besides the skinheads, I saw Teddy boys in drape jackets and crepe-soled shoes, bikers in leathers, a lot of mods in tight suits or parkas – some on scooters and some on foot – and also a motley assortment of punks, casuals and soon-to-be goths.

All these groups were parking and meeting up with their friends before parading up and down the seafront in packs, all the while showing off, eyeing up the other groups and bristling with youthful machismo. And at the same time, everyone was being closely monitored by the boys in blue.

The group of skinheads I was with quickly found a pub, The Hope, and established that as a base. I had no particular interest in spending all day drinking, so after taking a few photographs in the pub, I went outside and wandered around, just watching everything that was going on.

I could see that most of the Teds and the bikers were hanging around The Minerva, a short distance away from The Hope. Some of them were clearly not in the first flush of youth. Some could even have been veterans of the razor gangs of the Fifties or of the mods and rockers battles of the Sixties. They were a pretty tough-looking bunch. But, I found, just as happy to be photographed as the skinheads.

Within an hour of our arrival, the seafront had gone from being relatively sedate to appearing as crowded as Oxford Street just before Christmas.

DACOL FURNISHINGS LTD
QUALITY FURNITURE at DISCOUNT PRICES

66

JTO 397P

Southend, Easter Bank Holiday, 1979

ZONE
9 am-6 pm

Southend, Easter Bank Holiday, 1979

There was activity everywhere. From time to time there would be a bit of a commotion, with sirens and flashing blue lights alerting everyone that something was happening. And everyone in the vicinity would crane their necks to try to see what was going on. Then, after a while, another commotion would occur somewhere else, and off we'd go in a different direction. Occasionally I'd see some relatively inoffensive-looking lad being led away and put in the back of a police van whilst everyone else just carried on with their day.

The whole atmosphere was markedly tense and by lunch time the police clearly had their hands full.

Every so often, a detachment from one of the youth tribes would gather outside their pub and swagger down the front, getting as close to one of the other tribes as the police would allow. They would then just stand around scowling, trying to look threatening for a bit before walking back to their original location.

After a while, one of the other groups would do more or less the same thing. One could interpret it all as a form of street theatre that never quite got past the first act. Everyone seemed to be waiting for some sort of big, set-piece punch-up, which just never happened.

Occasionally, I'd see a group break into a run and dart up one of the side streets, during which a few tables and chairs or a postcard carousel or two might get pushed over. And some

families with young children, who were minding their own business, would go scurrying.

Not much more than that. None of the opposing tribes ever got close enough to actually engage one another and the runs would quickly peter out and disperse.

There was only the odd skirmish. Occasionally one group or another found an unsuspecting straggler who had yet to meet up with his friends. There would be a brief encounter

interested in portraiture than reportage anyway. Some of the skinheads were terrible show offs and I didn't want any resultant violence to be on my conscience.

Nevertheless, one policeman, a guy with a lot of gold braid on his cap, walked over at one point and said he'd arrest me if I didn't stop taking photographs. He didn't say why. I put my camera back in my bag for a bit and took it out again once he'd gone.

Most of the skinheads seemed to

ONE POLICEMAN, A GUY WITH A LOT OF GOLD BRAID ON HIS CAP, WALKED OVER AT ONE POINT AND SAID HE'D ARREST ME IF I DIDN'T STOP TAKING PHOTOGRAPHS.

involving fists and boots. It was all completely mindless, and the people at the back of the group wouldn't have had the first clue what was going on or why. But it didn't stop some of them wanting to run in and deliver a few cowardly kicks of their own. A police car would quickly turn up and everyone bar the straggler would scatter. The straggler would invariably be on the ground, a little battered and bruised but usually no worse than that. They all seemed to get to their feet okay afterwards.

Right from the start I decided not to photograph any fighting. I didn't like the idea that the presence of my camera might encourage someone to do something they might not do otherwise. I was always more

view the whole occasion as great fun. I couldn't quite understand that. No one really seemed to know what was happening, there was zero organisation and at no time did the skinheads appear to have a plan of action. They just spent the day in a big cheerful group, hanging around drinking. And they rather meekly allowed the police to direct and corral them all day.

By mid-afternoon, it seemed that the police had lost patience. They rounded up the group I'd come down with and escorted us all back to the station, where we were told to get on the next train and go home. I didn't see Wally on the way back; I think he'd managed to get himself arrested. As I eventually discovered, Wally usually did.

This spread: Southend, Easter Bank Holiday, 1979

This spread: Southend, Easter Bank Holiday, 1979

Walking down to the seafront, Southend, 1979

After going to Southend that day, over the next year or so I spent a lot of my spare time eagerly photographing and sometimes interviewing as many skinheads as I could.

I went to all the places, usually pubs, that they used as their meeting points in London. These included the Fountain in Deptford, the Governor General in Grove Park and the Crown & Shuttle and the White Horse in Shoreditch (until the skinheads got barred from the latter).

A lot of skinheads would also congregate in the area around Brick Lane on Sundays.

Most of them, at some point, would visit The Last Resort, a clothing store on Goulston Street, near Petticoat Lane. That eventually became the biggest skinhead hangout of them all.

On Saturday afternoons, some skins would meet up in Kings Road in Chelsea and, when it was nice, lounge around on Dovehouse Green.

Whenever bands popular with skinheads were playing, like The Specials AKA, Madness, Sham 69 or the band also called The Last Resort, I'd go to the gigs. Those would often be in places like The Electric Ballroom in Camden, The Hammersmith Palais

and The Bridge House in Canning Town.

I remember once, early one evening, I was walking along one of the streets in Camden behind The Electric Ballroom. I was with my girlfriend (now wife) Jo-Anne. A group of four skinheads ran up behind and jumped on me, nearly knocking me to the ground. It was supposed to be affectionate.

They were all skinheads I knew and it was just their particular way of saying hello. It certainly surprised Jo-Anne, who thought I was being attacked.

Chelsea, 1981

Chelsea, 1981

Top left: Governor General, Grove Park, 1979
Top right and centre: Hastings, 1981
Left: Richmond, 1980

Chelsea, 1981

At the 1980 show 'Skinheads' in Glebe Place, Chelsea

At the end of the year, I felt I had a decent set of photographs and some very apposite taped interviews.

It took me a long time to transcribe and edit all the tapes. I wanted to keep the flavour and emphasis of the skinheads' speech, yet ensure they were easily understandable when written down. I thought that

from some of my photos propped up in the background.

Called simply 'Skinheads', the show was a big success. Lots of people came to see it, some travelling quite a distance. I even saw coach parties of schoolchildren. I don't really know why, because the interviews contained a lot of bad language and I didn't edit

MY MOTHER CAME TO SEE THE SHOW AND TOLD ME THAT THERE WERE SOME SWEAR WORDS USED THAT SHE'D NEVER EVEN HEARD BEFORE.

transcribing word-for-word risked belittling them, so I tidied it up a little.

Somehow (I don't quite recall how), in September 1980 I got offered a show at the Chenil Studio Gallery in Chelsea. The artists Andrew Heard and David Robilliard helped find the space for me.* The show comprised my best 55 photos and selections from about a dozen of the interviews.

The show received an enormous amount of publicity and was reviewed in all the Sunday broadsheets and both London evening papers. I even got interviewed on the TV show *Check It Out*, with cardboard cutouts taken

any of that out. My mother came to see the show and told me that there were some swear words used that she'd never even heard before. (I did wonder how she knew they were swear words, but I didn't argue.)

Some days, when I dropped in to see how the show was doing, the place was actually crowded.

The exhibition certainly seemed to strike a chord. Most of the comments in the visitors book were favourable, but a couple of people asked why I'd only interviewed those skinheads with very extremist views?

That wasn't the case at all. Those were the only views I heard.

*Both now passed away. RIP.

This spread: The first British Movement march, Westminster, 1979

I didn't pick any of my interview subjects based on what I thought their views might be beforehand. It was simply down to the individual skinhead's willingness and availability to be interviewed. It was really the path of least resistance. They didn't all say yes.

When I assembled the material for my show, I was an amateur photographer. I was also very much an amateur interviewer as well. I just did my best. The fact that all my interview subjects seemed to speak with one voice was not by design.

On subjects like immigration, during the time I conducted my interviews, I simply did not hear anyone that didn't hold the same view.

Amazingly, this included a few black skinheads and one or two who appeared to be of mixed race or Asian. The non-white skinheads all expressed negative views about other non-white immigrant groups and indeed anyone who they seemed to view as further down the pecking order than themselves.

The pay-off was that the non-white skinheads all appeared to be accepted by the rest. Being a skinhead seemed to be most important. If, and only if, one was a skinhead, one's race and skin colour were apparently deemed less significant. Of course, when one asks ex-skinheads about this today,

they almost all say that the bigots were in a minority and they weren't part of that minority themselves.

Who am I to say this wasn't true? All I can say is that my interviews were an honest reflection of the views I heard at the time. The great writer and essayist Susan Sontag once wrote that "the photographer is not simply the person who records the past but someone who invents it". I can certainly see her point. Almost by

definition, one can't take a photograph or make a record of anything without expressing a point of view. As a documentary photographer one is constantly making choices and, afterwards, when it comes to edit, print and show the work, more choices have to be made.

My political and social views were not the same as any of my skinhead subjects. At the time I was involved in this work, I was also a Labour Party activist.

Nevertheless, I still wanted to do right by the skinheads because, like any of us, they deserved to have the truth told about them.

I didn't advertise my own views. They were irrelevant to the job in hand. But by the same token, I didn't lie to anyone. And for some reason they seemed pretty accepting of my having a different opinion from them. Very few of them ever tried to convert me to their viewpoint.

After my 'Skinhead' show closed, I continued to photograph the skinheads but on a much less frequent, more opportunistic basis.

ON SUBJECTS LIKE IMMIGRATION, DURING THE TIME I CONDUCTED MY INTERVIEWS, I SIMPLY DID NOT HEAR ANYONE THAT DIDN'T HOLD THE SAME VIEW.

In 1981, I got a commission from the US magazine *Rolling Stone* to shoot an article on skinheads and, though it ultimately only appeared in a very abbreviated form, this provided further impetus for me to continue. After that, I tended to only photograph skinheads when I happened upon them in the normal course of my photographic endeavours.

I also did quite a few press interviews and learnt, for the first but not the last time, that one's views are not always fairly represented by the media and sometimes journalists have a hidden agenda.

Hounslow bus station, 1980

Near Aldgate, 1980

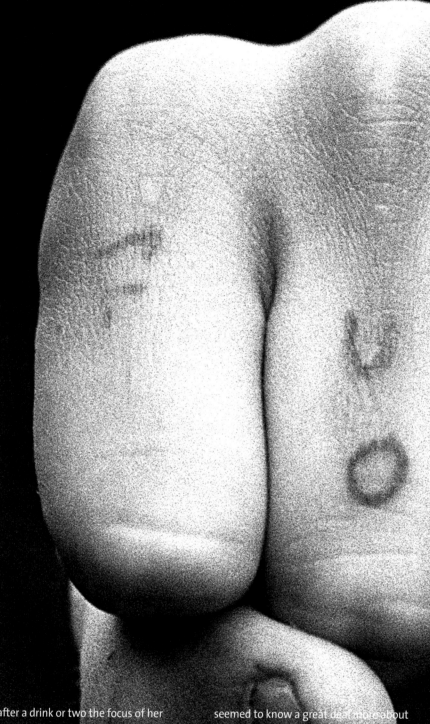

One evening a reporter from the *Observer* came to see me. She was young, blonde and attractive. She finished her interview with me and asked if I wanted to go for a drink in the bar across the road. She'd started out asking me a lot of fairly dumb questions about my show and skinheads in general, but after a drink or two the focus of her conversation turned to a couple of well known and somewhat notorious skinheads that I'd taken great care not to actually name myself. Somehow, during our drink, it dawned on me that she wasn't interested in me or my photographs at all and, furthermore, she seemed to know a great deal more about skinheads than she'd initially led me to believe.

She probably knew more than I did. I felt she'd simply been trying to dupe me into filling in a few of the blanks. Luckily, I don't drink much and the little I knew about the guys she was talking

Leicester Square, 1981

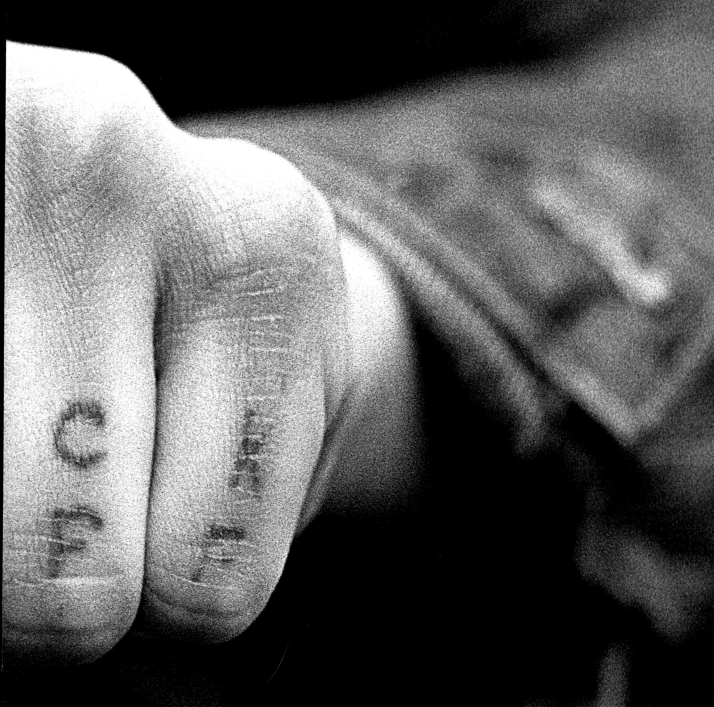

about would have been hearsay. Her ruse didn't work.

When the *Observer* article appeared, there was no mention of me or my show at all. As I had suspected, the article was about the two notorious skinheads, an affray and the supposed involvement of a far-right splinter group. I knew nothing about any of that stuff anyway, but afterwards I became a lot more wary.

The well-known pulp fiction author Richard Allen also came into my office. He told me he'd gone to see my show and had really liked it.

To this day I'm not sure exactly what he was after. I think he may have wanted to investigate the idea of using my photos for some sort of publishing project. He was a portly, balding Canadian in a beige mac and, all in all, I didn't find him too impressive. Maybe he thought the same about me because I never heard any more from him.

The famous fashion photographer Nick Knight, then a student, also came in. He turned up in my office dressed from head to toe in authentic skinhead gear, but there was something about him that made me think he wasn't quite the real deal. He was charming, intelligent and, even then, I could see he was an extremely talented photographer.

He had an idea for doing a book about skinheads with me, Ian McKell (another young photographer) and himself. I wasn't really interested. Nick struck me as being far too much of a fanboy. If I was ever going to do a book, and it was certainly an ambition, I wanted to do something that was more of an even-handed social document than the idea Nick outlined.

At the end of our meeting I concluded that Nick was a bit of a poser. I told him what I thought and it didn't go down too well but, to give him his due, he remained faultlessly polite.

I just didn't see how one could remain objective whilst also being (or pretending to be) a skinhead oneself? For me, this would indicate implicit approval. Or, at the very least, it would muddy the water.

That's not to criticise, in any way, Nick's work or that of Gavin Watson.* That way was fine for them, but it would not have been fine for me. In time, I came to realise that objectivity was pretty unattainable anyway, so maybe it would not have mattered.

But I don't think I could have been a skinhead then even if I'd wanted to be. Besides anything else, during the period 1979 – 1984, I was also photographing the Blitz Kids. I could hardly subsume myself into both groups simultaneously. It would have been shallow and patronising and, besides, my subjects would have seen through me in an instant.

As I already mentioned, when I was 15, I dabbled for a while with becoming a skinhead. Back then being a skinhead seemed to me to be all about the haircut, the clothes, the music, the girls and the fighting.

But, then again, isn't everything when one is a teenager?

their lot. And I didn't realise quite how deeply held and extreme their views were. In the fullness of time, I came to realise that they had an antipathy for anyone that wasn't exactly like them. This included the police, the "straights", any sort of authority. In fact, more or less the rest of society.

I reckon 95% of the skinheads I met were basically good kids with mixed up and misguided views. Often when they said they "hated" something I think the emotion they really felt was mistrust. Which one could understand in the context of their socio-demographic

WHEN I FIRST RAN INTO THEM IN 1979, I HAD ABSOLUTELY NO IDEA HOW PROFOUNDLY RESENTFUL THEY FELT ABOUT THEIR LOT.

The original skinhead clothes were basically just hard-wearing, fairly smart work-wear. The music was mostly American soul or Caribbean blue beat and ska – the sort of music that, even wearing big boots, was almost impossible not to get up and dance to. In the Sixties, skinheads had nothing to do with bigotry or right-wing politics. If anything, it seemed to me that black and Afro-Caribbean culture was very much admired by the skinheads of my teen years. Whenever possible they wanted to go to their clubs (like Soho's Flamingo), hang out with them and try to be like them.

I soon found out that this wasn't the case with the late Seventies skinheads. When I first ran into them in 1979, I had absolutely no idea how profoundly resentful they felt about

group. They often came from a white, working class that was myopic, insular and unwilling to mix with anyone that was not exactly like them. Add to that mix a poor education and a strong sense of entitlement and what could one expect?

In my interviews with the skinheads, one subject which came up time and again was their treatment at school.

Usually it seemed that they'd been treated without any respect, told they were stupid, ostracised, made to feel different, excluded and then often expelled. I heard this story repeatedly.

Their schooling, or lack of it, had left them with very limited opportunities and it was hard to see how many of them would really have much of a chance.

* This was a long time before I actually knew of Gavin Watson's work.

Chelsea, 1980

Chelsea, 1981

Despite everything, I still found that I couldn't help but like a lot of them. The vast majority were almost always polite and friendly and I suspect that some had real talent. As a photographer it's never been my desire to become friends with my subjects. I've actually always felt it was better if I didn't. I don't think one can do a good, honest job whilst worrying, even subconsciously, about the approval of one's subjects. But I certainly think one needs to be able to empathise.

In February 1981, I was fired from my job as an art director and I decided, mostly because of the great reaction to my 'Skinhead' show, to try to become a professional photographer.

Within 18 months I was working for some of the country's best-known magazines. In 1982 I started working for the music paper *NME* and was able to go back to my first love – photographing musicians.

I was soon travelling the world as a rock photographer and, by 1984, I no longer had the same amount of time to devote to documenting skinheads or any other youth group. And so my skinhead project came to a natural end. After 1984 I saw less and less of them around in London. Some of the ones I'd known had moved on, grown up and became parents of little skinheads themselves.

I really enjoyed photographing skinheads. At no time did I feel that they were all that much different from me. Strip away the cock-eyed social and political views and I felt there was a real connection.

And I thought they were the most photogenic youth cult of them all.

Among them there were some undeniably beautiful and memorable faces, some of the best faces I've ever photographed. And unlike the punks and the New Romantics, there was a real conviction there about what it meant to live a certain way of life. And about what it meant to be British. It never really looked like they were posing or dressing up, it never really seemed like it was just about the clothes. For some of them, being a skinhead was a way of life.

Contact sheet. Various, 1979

tHE PHOtOGRaPHS

Contact sheet. Various, 1979

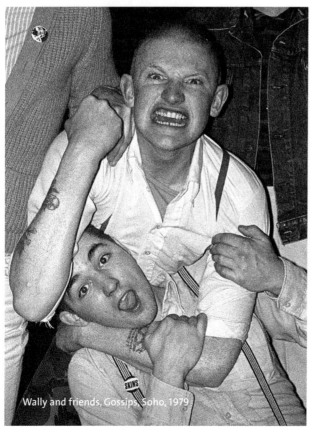

Wally and friends, Gossips, Soho, 1979

Wally gets arrested, Charing Cross station, 1979

FORD 115
TRANSIT

OLICE

Wally gets arrested, outside Charing Cross station, 1979

Chelsea, 1981

Outside the Crown and Shuttle, Shoreditch, 1979

Hastings, 1981

Chelsea, 1981

Outside the Chelsea Drugstore, 1980

Chris, Chelsea, 1981

Leicester Square, 1981

East London, 1980

This page: Brighton, 1980

Southend, 1979

This spread: Near Carnaby Street, 1980